FUTURE SOCIETIES

BY JOHN HAMILTON

Editor: Paul Joseph
Graphic Design: John Hamilton
Cover Design: Neil Klinepier
Cover Illustration: *The Ring* ©1986 Don Maitz
Interior Photos and Illustrations: p 1 *Day by Night* ©1980 Don Maitz; p 4 *The City and the Stars*, courtesy Signet Books; p 5 *None But Man* ©1976 Don Maitz; p 6 *Cyteen* ©1987 Don Maitz; p 7 *Cyteen II* ©1988 Don Maitz; p 9 *Out Where the Big Ships Go* ©1980 Don Maitz; p 10 *Nineteen Eighty-Four* opera, Corbis; p 11 *Dark City*, Corbis; p 12 (top) man walking past video surveillance, Corbis; p 12 (bottom) scene from *1984*, Corbis; p 13 (top) portrait of George Orwell, Corbis; p 13 (bottom) scene from *V for Vendetta*, Corbis; p 14 scene from *Logan's Run*, courtesy MGM; p 15 ID barcode on bald head, Corbis; p 16 computer hacker, Corbis; p 17 computer persona, Corbis; p 18 *Neuromancer*, courtesy Ace Science Fiction; p 19 *The Ring* ©1986 Don Maitz; p 20 spinner, courtesy Warner Bros.; p 21 (top left) Harrison Ford, Corbis; p 21 (top right) Daryl Hannah, Corbis; p 21 (bottom) Rutger Hauer, Corbis; p 22 (top) Joe Pantoliano, Corbis; p 22 (bottom) Carrie-Anne Moss, Corbis; p 23 (top) The Matrix group photo, courtesy Warner Bros.; p 23 (bottom) squiddies, courtesy Warner Bros.; p 24 scene from *Planet of the Apes*, Corbis; p 25 *Tamasara* ©1983 Don Maitz; p 27 alien city, Corbis; p 28 brain, Corbis; p 29 *Pretender* ©1984 Don Maitz.

Library of Congress Cataloging-in-Publication Data

Hamilton, John, 1959-
  Future societies / John Hamilton.
      p. cm. -- (The world of science fiction)
  Includes index.
  ISBN-13: 978-1-59679-988-2
  ISBN-10: 1-59679-988-9
  1. Science fiction--History and criticism--Juvenile literature. 2. Utopias in literature--Juvenile literature.
3. Dystopias in literature--Juvenile literature. I. Hamilton, John, 1959- World of science fiction. II. Title.

PN3433.6H36 2007
809.3'876209372--dc22

                        2006016391

CONTENTS

PEOPLE OF THE FUTURE

What a dreadful day to die, not nearly as nice as the last time, thought Alfred P. Jones III, head of the richest corporation in the galaxy, as he strolled toward the cloning vats.

A dreadful day to die? When is it ever a *good* day to die? And cloning vats? What on Earth are cloning vats?

What on Earth. Reading that paragraph, you quickly realize you're not on our planet anymore, or at least Earth as we know it today. One of science fiction's great strengths is its ability to describe possible future societies. These made-up societies serve as interesting background to a story's plot. But they can also be goals, or warnings of things to come.

In the example above, we can tell much about the fictional culture in just a few sentences. Apparently, people die quite often in this world. Alfred P. Jones, a very rich man, certainly wasn't all that upset about his own death. And what of the cloning vats? The answer to the mystery, perhaps, is that for some reason people die over and over, but are then reborn as clones. Is this a good thing? Or is the story a warning of what our world will become unless we change our ways? Science fiction author Arthur C. Clarke wrote a novel in 1956, *The City and the Stars*, which mirrors this same idea. In the book, a society of the far future is run by a huge central computer, which stores people's minds in its memory. When people die, the computer creates another body and then "downloads" the person's mind into it. Farfetched? Perhaps, but the story is a way for us to examine our place in the world, to find out what it means to be part of the human race.

Facing page: None But Man, by Don Maitz.
Below: Arthur C. Clarke's *The City and the Stars.*

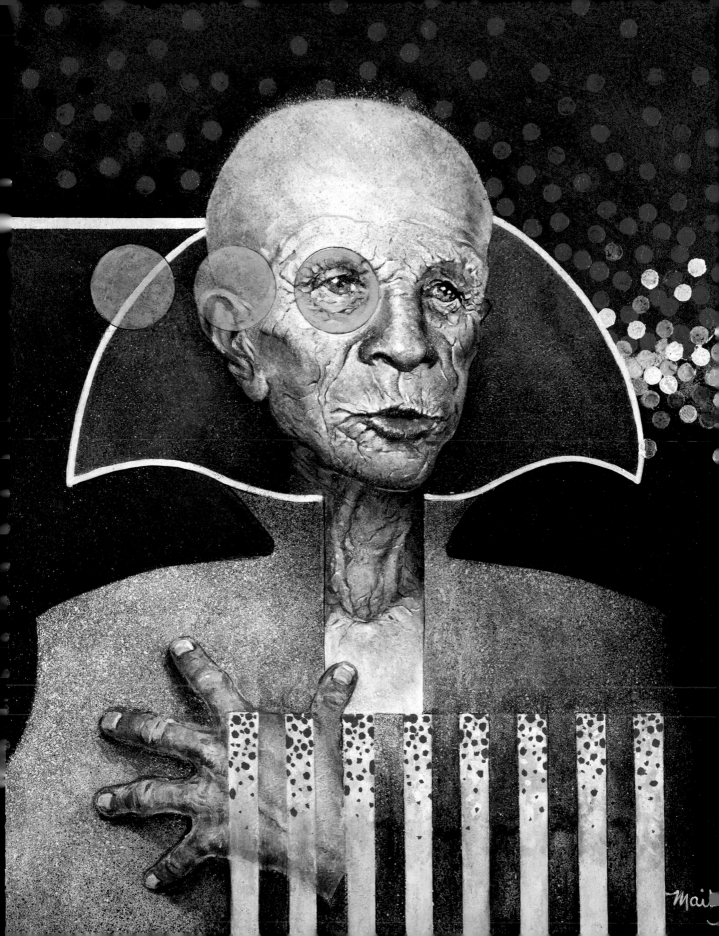

Science fiction authors usually set out to create interesting and realistic views of the future. But a future society can also be created that is meant to be a satire, which is a humorous way of pointing out the shortcomings of our current culture. A common technique used by science fiction writers is to take a small part of our current culture and then exaggerate it, creating a future society that seems to have gone crazy. For example, in the 1952 novel *The Space Merchants*, by Frederik Pohl and C. M. Kornbluth, the earth's governments are replaced by corporations and advertising agencies. In David Mitchell's *Cloud Atlas*, a future fast-food restaurant employs a hologram of a man called Papa Song, who entertains customers and gives pep-talks to the employees.

Future societies in science fiction come in all shapes and sizes. Some are hopeful, but many are pessimistic. Others are simply entertaining, or puzzling, or just plain weird. In the end, though, they all serve the same purpose: to hold a mirror up to our own civilization, and make us think.

Below: Cyteen, by Don Maitz.
Facing page: Cyteen II, by Don Maitz.

7

UTOPIAS

A utopia is an imaginary place where everything is perfect. The name comes from the book *Utopia*, written in 1516 by Sir Thomas More, about a fictional island and its seemingly perfect society. In a utopia, people are equal, nobody's poor, there is no war, and everybody gets along. In a nutshell, everyone is just basically happy. The word utopia is a combination of two Greek words, *ou* and *topos*. Put together, it literally means "nowhere," or "no-place." A utopia is an ideal, a place that doesn't really exist— but everyone wishes it did.

Science fiction sometimes explores the theme of utopias, but it isn't as common today as it was in the late 19th century through the 1940s and 1950s. The most famous utopia from this period isn't even science fiction. Shangri-La is a mystical valley hidden amidst the Himalaya Mountains. Described in James Hilton's 1933 novel, *Lost Horizon*, Shangri-La is a land where people are always happy and content, sheltered from the corruption of the outside world.

In modern science fiction, utopias are usually represented by world-wide governments that form a protective umbrella over their societies. Sometimes these societies are run by the unemotional minds of advanced computers or robots. This is an optimistic future, where science and technology have taken away many of the hardships that plague mankind today. Several of Arthur C. Clarke's novels, such as *Imperial Earth*, feature such societies. The universe of *Star Trek* is another example. In most modern science fiction utopias, however, even though problems like war and racism have been eliminated or drastically reduced, other troubles remain that must still be grappled with, such as drug abuse or the ethical problems of cloning or bio-engineering. Even in science fiction, there is no perfect, ideal place.

Facing page: Out Where the Big Ships Go, by Don Maitz.

DYSTOPIAS

Welcome to the dark side of science fiction: dystopia. Basically, a dystopia is the opposite of a utopia. It's a fictional place where almost everything is bad or unpleasant, where an oppressive government spies on its citizens, where personal freedom is severely limited, and the environment is unhealthy or downright toxic. In short, a dystopia is a pretty nasty place in which to live.

English philosopher John Stuart Mills first used the term dystopia in 1868. The word literally means "bad place." It's not quite accurate to say that a dystopia is the *exact* opposite of a utopia. In many stories, the culture seems perfect, filled with shiny, happy people. The government, or religion, or whoever is running the society, seems to have everything under tight control. But in a dystopia, when you scratch the surface of the society, you see an ugly truth underneath. It's a world turned upside down, a false utopia, a prison disguised as a paradise. Social control is too tight, which leads to terror. Real personal freedom is nonexistent, and anyone who speaks up in protest is "eliminated." Governments like this are called totalitarian. They demand total obedience from their citizens—or else.

Facing page: A scene from the 1998 film, *Dark City.*
Below: A scene from a 2005 opera version of George Orwell's *Nineteen Eighty-Four.*

Above: A man under the watchful eyes of a totalitarian society.
Below: A scene from *1984*.

A story featuring a dystopia is a warning of what will happen if bad trends in society continue. It became a popular theme in science fiction after World War II, in the late 1940s. The world had seen the horrors inflicted on people during the totalitarian governments of Nazi Germany and the Stalin-led Soviet Union. Dystopia stories were a way of reflecting the fears many people had of the direction they saw the world turning.

In 1949, George Orwell wrote the novel *Nineteen Eighty-Four*, about a future totalitarian society with an all-seeing government called Big Brother, and Thought Police who use psychology and secret surveillance to arrest and eliminate anyone who even thinks of challenging authority. George Orwell used fiction to warn people of future trends that he foresaw. *Nineteen Eighty-Four* used extreme examples to make its point, but some people see real-life parallels in today's "war on terrorism," a conflict with no end, where the U.S. government spies on its own citizens, and many consider it unpatriotic to criticize the leadership. If advanced technology made Thought Police a reality, would our government use it? Alan Moore's comic book series of the 1980s, *V for Vendetta*, explored many of these same disturbing themes.

Stories of dystopia in science fiction have many things in common. Usually, there is a background of disaster. Something horrific has happened to change society, either a war, overpopulation, or perhaps a natural disaster. A government, or some other authority, like the Church, steps in to restore order. In many stories, the lower and middle class are very poor, living in extreme hardship, while the upper, or ruling, class of people are well-off. The government brings a sense of order and safety to society, but at a price: people lose their freedom. Then, there is a hero, a protagonist, who questions society, investigates, and finds that there is something terribly, terribly wrong. The hero sets out to change society, but the ruling class tries to stop him at all costs.

Above: George Orwell, author of *Nineteen Eighty-Four.*
Below: Actress Natalie Portman in a scene from *V for Vendetta.*

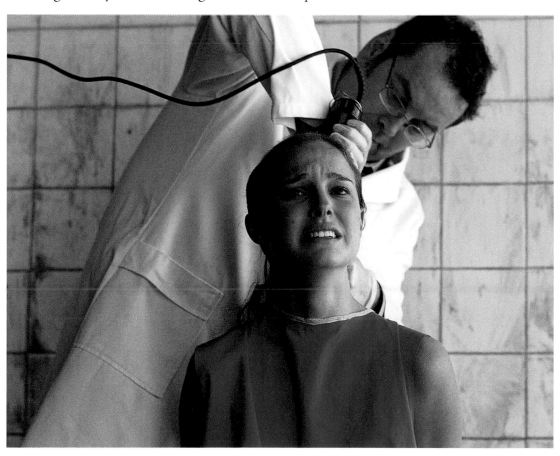

Logan's Run, a novel published in 1967 by William F. Nolan and George Clayton, is a typical example of a dystopian-themed science fiction story. (The book was made into a movie in 1976.) In the 23rd century, people live in a perfect society where everyone can find fulfillment and pleasure. There's only one catch: a fear of overpopulation means that anyone reaching a certain age (twenty-one in the book) must be put to death. People have crystals embedded in their palm that turn black when they reach "last-day," the day they are to be killed by a special police force called the Sandmen. Rather than submit to this enforced euthanasia, some people become "runners." They flee the Sandmen and seek out Sanctuary, a rumored shelter where people can grow old in defiance of society.

In the story, Logan 5 is a Sandman who becomes a runner on purpose in order to find and destroy Sanctuary. He teams up with a companion, Jessica 6, and together they search out the fabled Sanctuary. During their adventure, Logan 5 learns the evils of his society, and decides to become a runner for real.

Dystopia comes from the fears of the age in which it is written. Today, people have many fears besides Big Brother. They worry about environmental disasters, poverty, disease, bio-engineering, and the rapid impact of advanced technology, such as computers and the media. Modern science fiction reflects these fears, warning of troubles to come, and offering solutions before it's too late.

Right: A scene from the 1976 film, *Logan's Run.*
Facing page: A man has an ID tattooed on his scalp. Many people worry that today's advances in technology will result in a loss of privacy.

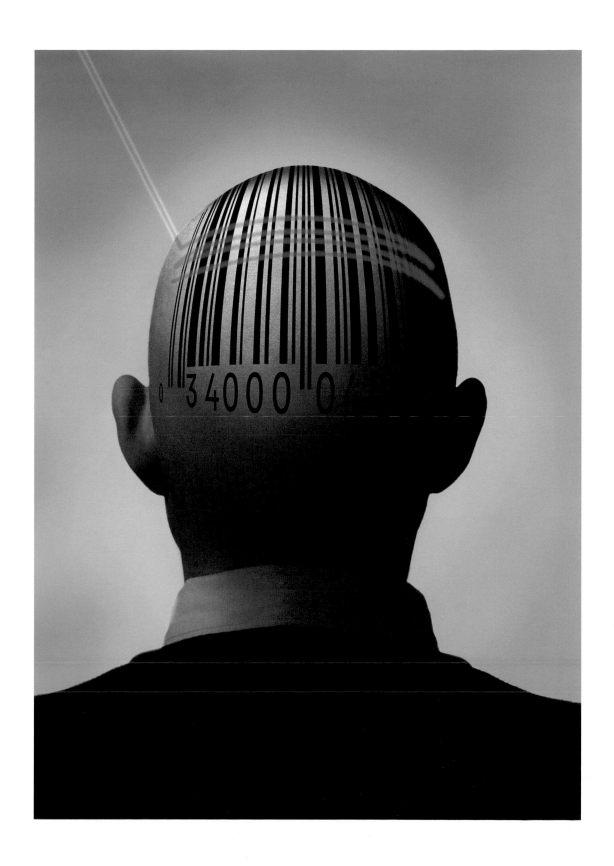

CYBERPUNK

In the early 1980's, a fresh category of science fiction surfaced. It merged visions of near-future dystopia with a new group of youth who had grown up with computers and knew the language of technology. In 1983, Bruce Bethke published a short story called "Cyberpunk" in the magazine *Amazing Science Fiction*. The title of the story referred to a group of teenage hackers, with bad attitudes, who broke into the Internet to steal money, wipe out bank accounts, and even erase people's jobs.

The word cyberpunk is a combination of the words punk and cybernetics, which is the science of control and communication of both machines and living creatures. Originally, it was meant to describe antisocial rebels who use computers to commit their crimes. Nowadays, cyberpunk more commonly refers to a tech-savvy hero who fights back, using the system against itself.

Facing page: A human "persona" that exists inside the memory of a computer.
Below: A computer hacker tries to break into a secure network.

Cyberpunk usually takes place in a frightening, troubled future society. Common elements include Internet use (and abuse), mega-corporations, artificial intelligence (with machines that think like humans), and a society where the social order has broken down. In cyberpunk stories, technology grows into ultra-technology; people and machines merge to become one.

This can include a computer hacker using virtual reality goggles to cruise cyberspace (a computer-simulated reality), or a robot that is so complex it is almost impossible to tell the difference between it and a real human.

Cyberpunk stories have a bleak, gritty style. Danger is always just around the next corner. Many people compare cyberpunk to detective stories with hard-bitten private investigators, or to the crime movies of the 1940s and 1950s called "film noir." (*Film noir* is a French term that means "black film.") Examples include *The Maltese Falcon*, or Orson Welles' 1958 film, *Touch of Evil*. Cyberpunk usually features a similar kind of hard-boiled anti-hero, a loner who operates outside of the "system."

Facing page: The Ring, by Don Maitz.
Below: William Gibson's *Neuromancer.*

Cyberpunk novels became very popular in the 1980s. The genre's most famous authors include William Gibson, Rudy Rucker, Bruce Sterling, and Neal Stephenson. The publication of Gibson's 1984 novel, *Neuromancer*, is often called the true starting point of the cyberpunk trend in science fiction.

Neuromancer is the story of Charles Case, a brilliant "cyber-cowboy" who hacks into the digital world of cyberspace to help free an artificial intelligence (AI) named Wintermute. The AI seeks to escape into an Internet-like computer network called the matrix. Once there, Wintermute wants to fuse with another AI called Neuromancer, in order to become a superintelligence that is part of the matrix itself. Assisting Case on his mission is Molly, a "Razorgirl" who has modified her body to include retractable knife blades under her fingernails, and lens implants in her eye sockets that give her enhanced vision.

Neuromancer was a ground-breaking novel that explored many ideas about technology before they became popular, including virtual reality, artificial intelligence, and cyberspace. It won the Nebula Award in 1984 and the Hugo Award in 1985.

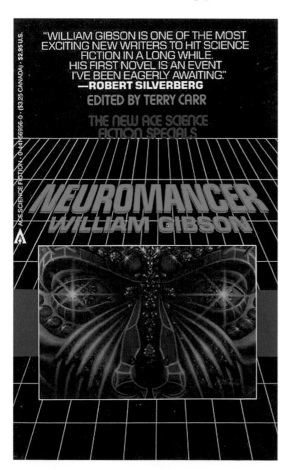

"WILLIAM GIBSON IS ONE OF THE MOST EXCITING NEW WRITERS TO HIT SCIENCE FICTION IN A LONG WHILE. HIS FIRST NOVEL IS AN EVENT I'VE BEEN EAGERLY AWAITING."
—ROBERT SILVERBERG

EDITED BY TERRY CARR

THE NEW ACE SCIENCE FICTION SPECIALS

NEUROMANCER
WILLIAM GIBSON

Blade Runner was one of the first science fiction films to include elements of what today we call cyberpunk. Released in 1982, the film is based on Philip K. Dick's 1968 novel, *Do Androids Dream of Electric Sheep?* In fact, many of Dick's novels have cyberpunk themes. Published years before cyberpunk was a recognized genre, his books often feature societies in decay, artificial intelligence, and a blurring of reality and illusion.

Blade Runner is set in a near-future dystopia of urban Los Angeles, in the year 2019. The city is a grimy, dangerous place. Many people have moved off the planet, to safer "off-world colonies." Those left behind live in places that are overcrowded and polluted. Most animals have become extinct. They are now genetically manufactured by private companies. Going one step further, the Tyrell Corporation creates biologically based androids, called replicants, which are almost completely identical to their human counterparts. Replicants are grown to serve as slaves, especially as workers in hazardous mining colonies in space.

If a replicant escapes into the city, it is considered a hazard to humans. Rick Deckard, played by Harrison Ford, is a Blade Runner, a kind of policeman whose job is to hunt down runaway replicants. The story begins when several of the most advanced replicants—Nexus 6 models—escape from an off-world colony and return to Earth. Deckard's job is to find and "retire" them. In other words, he's hired to legally kill the replicants.

Right: In *Blade Runner*, police travel in hovercars called "spinners."

Above: Daryl Hannah plays the replicant Pris in *Blade Runner.*
Left: Harrison Ford, as Rick Deckard, surveys a crime scene after "retiring" a replicant.
Below: Roy Batty, played by Rutger Hauer, is an advanced Nexus 6 replicant.

Meanwhile, the escaped replicants hide in the swirling chaos of the nightmarish Los Angeles. They are a superior breed of android, with memories implanted in their cybernetic brains to make them seem human—"More human than human," boasts the Tyrell Corporation. The Nexus 6 models have a built-in safeguard—a four-year lifespan—to keep them from overthrowing their human masters. The leader of the renegade replicants, Roy Batty (played by Rutger Hauer) desperately seeks out his creator, Dr. Eldon Tyrell, in order to receive a longer life.

Blade Runner is very dark and thoughtful, especially for such an action-oriented film. It explores many themes common to cyberpunk, including technology run amok, the nature of reality, and what it means to be human. It won the Hugo Award in 1983, a year after Philip K. Dick's death.

Above: Joe Pantoliano as Cypher, in *The Matrix.*
Below: Trinity, played by Carrie-Anne Moss, uses her martial arts skills against her enemies.

A more recent example of a cyberpunk film is 1999's *The Matrix,* and its two sequels, *The Matrix Reloaded* and *The Matrix Revolutions,* both released in 2003. *The Matrix* is a disturbing story about intelligent machines that enslave humans and use them unwittingly as a source of power. The super-computers use robots in their war against humanity. The enslaved humans are fooled into thinking they are living normal lives. In reality, the machines physically plug the humans' brains into a vast computer network, creating an artificial reality, an illusion called the "Matrix." The Matrix is a simulated world in which humans have no knowledge of the war between people and computers.

Groups of freedom fighters manage to unplug their brains from the Matrix, and then fight against the machines. The hero of the film, Neo, played by Keanu Reeves, is a brilliant computer hacker within the simulated reality of the Matrix. He is chosen to become "The One."

Neo is a human who can enter the Matrix with his mind and destroy the computer slave-masters. Like many cyberpunk heroes, Neo begins the story as a loner who is an expert with computers. By story's end, he has seen the evil of his society and sets out to make things right, even though he's reluctant at first. The artificial intelligences that control the Matrix, naturally, do everything in their power to make Neo fail, but his skills and determination prove too strong in the end, and humanity is freed from its technological slavery.

Above, left to right: Joe Pantoliano as Cypher; Laurence Fishburne as Morpheus; Keanu Reeves as Neo; and Carrie-Anne Moss as Trinity, in *The Matrix.*

Left: The computer mind of the Matrix often uses killer robots called squiddies to hunt down human rebels.

POST-APOCALYPSE

At the end of World War III, will the survivors envy the dead? If the earth becomes a scorched cinder, or flesh-eating germs float on every breath of wind, would there be anything left to live for?

An apocalypse is a catastrophe that causes complete destruction on a worldwide scale. "Post" means "after." Post-apocalypse science fiction shows what kind of society would arise after a global disaster. These stories are often about groups of resourceful people who struggle for survival. If they're lucky, they manage to salvage what's left of their humanity and set out to rebuild civilization, usually a wiser society that's learned from the mistakes of the past. In many other stories, however, the future is much more bleak, with lessons learned too late.

Planet of the Apes is a novel published by Pierre Boulle in 1968. That same year, it was turned into a movie starring Charlton Heston. The book and movie differ in many places, but share the same basic plot. A group of astronauts lands on a planet in the far-future. It appears to be Earth-like, with one major exception: humans are enslaved by a complex society of intelligent apes. In the film version, the hero discovers that mankind has nearly wiped itself out because of a nuclear war, leaving the apes to evolve intelligence, enslave the remaining humans, and rule the earth.

Mad Max is a 1979 post-apocalypse film starring Mel Gibson. It takes place in an Australia of the near future, after the world has suffered wars and severe fuel shortages. Max is a police officer who tries to maintain law-and-order. He battles predatory motorized gangs in the Outback. The movie had a very low budget, but its frightening view of the future hit a nerve with audiences. It spawned two sequels: 1981's *The Road Warrior*, and 1985's *Mad Max Beyond Thunderdome*.

Facing page: Tamasara, by Don Maitz.
Below: A scene from *Planet of the Apes.*

ALIEN SOCIETIES

In science fiction, societies of the future aren't always human, of course. Alien societies have always been a big part of science fiction. *Star Wars* and *Star Trek* are littered with a multitude of interesting alien races. Besides their obvious physical differences, like bug-eyes, or antennas, or claws, aliens often have societies much different from humans. Sometimes alien cultures can be bizarre, or so different from us that we can't understand them at all. But that's part of their appeal—alien societies help give science fiction a "sense of wonder," which is what makes the genre so exciting.

Aliens in science fiction blend human imagination with scientific fact. Writers love to create alien societies because it's a way to explore our own culture. Aliens are really humans in disguise. In storytelling, aliens can take the place of human beings. They are a way for science fiction authors to talk about controversial issues like abortion, sexism, or human rights. It's easier to examine tough problems and think about solutions if the problems are happening to an alien society. Aliens can act like a mirror for our own human faults.

Alien societies are also used by science fiction authors to explore literary themes. In Polish author Stanislaw Lem's 1961 novel, *Solaris*, astronauts discover an ocean planet that may be the massive, collective "brain" of an alien civilization. The book raises questions about how we label consciousness, intelligence, and even life itself.

Facing page: Bat-winged aliens populate a city on a far-away planet.

THE FAR FUTURE

Imagine if we could somehow transport ourselves into the far future, not mere hundreds of years from now, but thousands, even millions of years. What would society be like? Would it be radically different? If we looked in a mirror, would we even recognize ourselves as human?

For more than 100 years, science fiction writers and filmmakers have been guessing about societies of the far future. The rise of technology, and the great strides of medicine and genetic engineering, have sparked the imaginations of countless writers and artists. Will we be a race of identical clones, each genetically "programmed" according to some sort of master plan? Or will the future be messier than that sterile vision?

Stories of medical advances that transform humanity are as old as Mary Shelley's 1818 novel, *Frankenstein*, or H. G. Wells' *The Island of Dr. Moreau*, the 1896 novel of a mad doctor who combines humans with animals. In the far future, will society demand that unpleasant, dangerous births be conducted in test tubes, with babies grown and incubated by machines? Will we be harvested from vats of ooze rather than grown inside the wombs of loving mothers?

Facing page: Pretender, by Don Maitz.
Below: A disembodied brain.

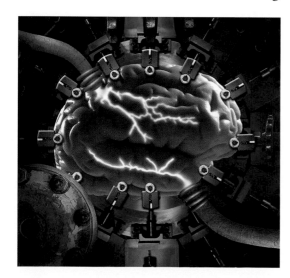

Venturing even further into the future, some science fiction authors think we'll eventually outgrow the need for our own bodies. Perhaps we'll be disembodied brains talking to each other telepathically from colorful liquid-filled jars, much like the Providers in the 1966 *Star Trek* episode, "The Gamesters of Triskelion." Hopefully, human evolution won't take us down that road. But in the world of science fiction, anything can happen.

GLOSSARY

ANDROID
A kind of robot that mimics people, both in appearance and behavior. In the film *Blade Runner*, replicants are a type of android.

ARTIFICIAL INTELLIGENCE
A computer that is so advanced that it mimics human thought. Also referred to as AI.

BIO-ENGINEERING
Using advanced technology to make a person "better" biologically. For example, future soldiers might be made stronger, with better eyesight and increased stamina.

CLONE
An organism that is "grown" from donor cells, making an exact copy of the original.

CYBERSPACE
A "virtual" reality that exists only inside the interconnected networks of advanced computers. The Internet is often called cyberspace.

GALAXY
A system of millions, or even hundreds of billions, of stars and planets, clustered together in a distinct shape, like a spiral or ellipse. Our Earth is located within the Milky Way Galaxy.

GENRE
A type, or kind, or a work of art. In literature, a genre is distinguished by a common subject, theme, or style. Some genres include science fiction, fantasy, and mystery.

HACKER
A criminal who illegally breaks into computer networks in order to steal information, or destroy and alter data files.

NAZI GERMANY

The Nazi political party came into power in Germany in 1933. Led by Adolf Hitler, the Nazis stressed national pride, political aggression, and racism, especially against Jews. The Nazi's totalitarian rule eventually led to World War II. After Germany's defeat in 1945, the Nazi party was abolished.

OVERPOPULATION

Having too many people for the planet to support. Overpopulation is a common problem in many science fiction stories.

PROTAGONIST

The main character in a story, usually the hero.

SATIRE

Using humor or exaggeration to point out and criticize people's stupidity. Satire is often used to criticize politics, but it is also used in literature such as science fiction.

STALIN, JOSEPH

The leader of the former Soviet Union from the 1920s until his death in 1953. Stalin's strong rule helped his country defeat Germany in World War II, but his totalitarian government caused the deaths of many thousands of innocent people.

TERRORISM

Using force and fear to weaken an opponent, such as by killing innocent civilians to make a political statement. The 2001 attacks on the World Trade Center and the Pentagon were acts of terrorism.

TOTALITARIAN

A kind of government, run by one political party, that is undemocratic and oppressive toward its citizens. Science fiction dystopias are often run by totalitarian governments.

INDEX